ISBN 978-1-334-26777-2
PIBN 10746136

English
Français
Deutsche
Italiano
Español
Português

www.forgottenbooks.com

Mythology Photography **Fiction**
Fishing Christianity **Art** Cooking
Essays Buddhism Freemasonry
Medicine **Biology** Music **Ancient
Egypt** Evolution Carpentry Physics
Dance Geology **Mathematics** Fitness
Shakespeare **Folklore** Yoga Marketing
Confidence Immortality Biographies
Poetry **Psychology** Witchcraft
Electronics Chemistry History **Law**
Accounting **Philosophy** Anthropology
Alchemy Drama Quantum Mechanics
Atheism Sexual Health **Ancient History**
Entrepreneurship Languages Sport
Paleontology Needlework Islam
Metaphysics Investment Archaeology
Parenting Statistics Criminology
Motivational

STATION BULLETIN 435   NOVEMBER 1956

The Influence of Waste Bark
on Plant Growth

By Stuart Dunn

SUPPLEMENT

The Comparative Value of Bark
as a Surface Mulch for Apples, Blueberries,
and Raspberries

By L. P. LATIMER

Acknowledgements

The experimental work herein reported was made possible by a research grant from the Brown Company, Berlin, New Hampshire. The planning and supervision of the project was the responsibility of a supervisory committee consisting of the following: L. T. Kardos, Agronomy Department, Chairman; Stuart Dunn, Botany Department; L. P. Latimer, Horticulture Department; Lewis Swain, Forestry Department; G. P. Percival, Agricultural and Biological Chemistry Department; and Edward Katz, Bacteriology Department. Most of the work of caring for greenhouse cultures of plants and field plots was done by L. P. Wolfe, Jr., and W. A. MacDonald.

The Influence of Waste Bark on Plant Growth

By STUART DUNN

Plant Physiologist
New Hampshire Agricultural Experiment Station

Introduction

MANY pulp and paper manufacturers, including the Brown Company, Berlin, New Hampshire, have to dispose of several tons of fresh bark produced at the mill every day. Present practice is to truck it away and dump it. This necessitates the use of trucks, grading equipment and labor. Experiments, therefore, were started in an effort to discover, if possible, a profitable outlet for waste bark, including possible benefits to agriculture through soil improvement.

A search of the literature reveals that very little work has been done on the effects of bark from pulpwood on soil and plants. Very little has been published on the subject. Rettie and Simmons (6) report that water-soaked bark, as it comes from the barking drums, contains upwards of 80 percent moisture. In this condition the fuel value is almost nil. Other reviews (5) indicate that bark may have possible industrial uses as well as soil building potentialities.

Studies with sawdust (1, 3, 4, 7) applied either directly to soil or as compost show that when well decomposed it may in either case benefit plant growth.

The experimental work with bark may be divided into two parts: (1) that dealing with greenhouse pot and bench cultures, and (2) field plot trials, and will be considered in that order.

Part I   Greenhouse Cultures

Effects on Plant Growth of Various Ratios of Bark to Soil and of Peat to Soil

An attempt was made to determine what proportion of bark or peat mixed with soil is necessary for optimum plant growth, compared to soil alone as control. Peat was used in this and many subsequent tests because it is a standard merchantable organic material used as a soil improver, and bark would have to compete with it in the market. The bark materials used were of four types: new softwood bark, new hardwood bark, old softwood bark, and old hardwood bark. The term 'new' means that the bark was fresh from the mill; the term 'old' means that it had been standing in piles for several years and was partly weathered and decomposed. Some of this latter material was in a fine powdery condition. The concentrations used for each of these and for peat were 10, 30, and 50 percent by volume as shown in Table 1. Each was thoroughly mixed with soil in these proportions. Enough of each mixture was prepared to fill 10 pails of 14-quart capacity. These pails were previously coated on the inside with a waterproof varnish.

Table 1. Average Yields (Grams) of Three Successive Crops: Bark-soil, Peat-soil Mixtures, and Soil Controls

Percent Organic Matter	Treatment	Cabbage Dry Wt. of Tops	Radish Fr. Wt. of Roots	Corn Dry Wt. of Tops
	Old softwood bark	18.8*	73.0	10.8
	Old hardwood bark	16.2†	89.3	11.2
10	Peat	14.3	88.1	11.3
	New hardwood bark	13.3	70.7	11.2
	New softwood bark	12.0	58.8	11.0
	Old softwood bark	17.0*	15.2	11.5
	Old hardwood bark	15.3	7.1	12.0
30	Peat	12.2	96.7‡	11.6
	New hardwood bark	5.5	23.5	11.9
	New softwood bark	3.6	12.9	12.2
	Old softwood bark	14.6	1.7	14.0
	Old hardwood bark	11.6	3.6	12.8
50	Peat	10.0	70.9	14.9
	New hardwood bark	2.3	8.3	12.1
	New softwood bark	1.3	4.9	11.7
	Soil only — Control	14.1	123.6	12.3

* Mean of yields significantly greater than controls at the 1 percent level.
† Mean of yield significantly greater than controls at the 5 percent level.
‡ Control not significantly greater at the 1 percent level.

Three successive crops were grown in these mixtures in the following order: (a) cabbage, one plant per pail; (b) radish, four plants per pail; and (c) field corn (Kingscrost), two plants per pail. About midway in the growth of the cabbage, a nutrient solution was supplied to correct deficiencies. Subsequent crops received fertilizer when soil tests indicated their need. Between the radish and corn crops the mixtures and soils were allowed to remain fallow for 6 months.

The yield results appear in Table 1. There are several noteworthy points. (1) Cabbage was the only crop showing yields significantly greater for bark than for the soil controls; two of those yields were for old softwood bark and one for old hardwood bark. The generally more advanced state of decomposition and finer texture of these old barks compared to new bark was probably largely responsible for this. Yields for plants in peat-soil mixtures were close to that for the control. (2) With increasing concentration of organic matter, the growth of cabbage was consistently poorer. (3) At the 30 percent concentration and above, except for the old softwood bark, there was no advantage in the use of bark or peat. (4) In the new barks, growth was very poor at the 30 and 50 percent levels of concentration.

With the radish crop all yields in bark or peat mixtures were much lower than the controls. However, the plants in the peat mixtures at the two higher proportions of 30 and 50 percent yielded much better than those in the corresponding proportions of any of the bark mixtures.

With the corn crop, growth in all the cultures was very uniform. Statistical analysis showed no significant variations from the controls. The decay of the organic matter during two previous crops, plus a fallow period, was probably largely responsible for this. There was a slight tendency for the growth of plants in the 50 percent mixtures to be better than in the 10 percent mixtures. The fact that the plants of the two previous crops in the 50 percent mixtures had been poorest of those grown in any of the three proportions of organic matter indicates that, even in this highest concentration, decay was well advanced.

Effect of Bark and Peat on Flower Production by Ornamentals

A snapdragon crop was grown in benches, followed later by a carnation crop. Three standard greenhouse benches were prepared in the following manner:

Bench No. 3 — Regular greenhouse compost made up of manure, soil, sand, and plant waste.

Bench No. 4 — A mixture of peat (25 percent) and greenhouse compost (75 percent) by volume.

Bench No. 11 — As above, except that 25 percent old hardwood bark was used in place of peat.

All of the materials in each bench were thoroughly mixed and steam sterilized. Tests showed sufficient nutrient present and pH levels satisfactory in all benches (6.0 to 6.6).

Snapdragon plants were set out in the benches on December 5, 1950. Each bench contained three varieties as listed in Table 2. All plants had been pinched because of their size when transplanted. No fertilizer was applied at this time nor during the experiment. On February 19, 1951, more than a year later, the first harvest was made. At this time and at each cutting for the following two weeks, the greatest number of flowers was harvested from the bench containing bark. In succeeding harvests the number of flowers cut from each bench tended to become equal. The total yields given in Table 2 show greatest production for the bark, next largest

Table 2. Total Yields of Flower Harvest from Greenhouse Beds

	Treatment		
	Bark ¼, Soil ¾	Peat ¼, Soil¾	Soil Only
Snapdragons — Variety			
White Wonder	246	225	205
Yellow Ethyl	239	208	202
Pink Peggy Schoroman	279	223	204
Total of all varieties	764	656	611
Carnations — Variety			
Cardinal	225	223	213
Harlequin	261	285	281

for peat and lowest for soil (compost mixture). Records were taken also on the length of flower stalks. The averages were: bark 61.3 cm., peat 77.6 cm., and soil 78.2 cm.

After the final snapdragon harvest, the contents of each bench were steam sterilized without moving them. Four varieties of carnation transplants were installed in equal numbers per bench. The varieties are listed, together with a summary of total yields of flowers in Table 2. Here the greatest total yield was given by the plants growing in the peat mixture, but probably none of the differences is very significant.

Apparently, in a highly organic compost mixture, such as the basic material used here, relatively little benefit was secured from additional organic matter such as peat or bark. However, bark might have some advantage in not rotting as quickly as many organic materials now in general use in greenhouse composts.

In connection with this work on ornamentals, mention may be made of a small experiment on orchids. Three orchid plants were planted in old hardwood bark on January 15, 1952. Nothing else was added. On December 15, 1952, these plants appeared to be perfectly healthy, and two of them had produced flowers. Old bark may be regarded as a satisfactory medium for orchid growing.

Comparative Effects of Bark and Other Wood Wastes on Plant Growth

Since considerable experimentation has been done with sawdust and other woodwastes (1, 3, 4, 7), it seemed of interest to compare plant growth in bark with several of these. The materials tested in this comparison are listed in Table 3. Ten one-gallon size cans were filled with each material. They were used in the pure state, i.e., no soil was mixed with the organic substances. A good loam potting soil was used as control. At the beginning of the experiment 10 grams of 5-10-10 fertilizer was applied to each can.

Two crops were grown: cabbage, one plant per can, followed by barley, fifteen plants per can. Between crops the contents of all the cans for each kind of material were re-mixed together and 3.5 grams of fertilizer added per can. The yields, as given in Table 3, show that plants grew much better

Table 3. Average Dry Weights (Grams) of Two Crops Grown In Waste Bark and Other Woodwastes

Treatment	Cabbage, Mean Dry Wt. of 10 Plants	Barley, Mean Dry Wt. of 9 Cans 15 Plants/Can
Old hardwood bark	7.8*	5.4*
Old softwood bark	7.1*	4.1*
½ sawdust, ½ old softwood bark	7.0*	3.2
Soil control	5.1	2.8
½ shavings, ½ silage	3.2	7.0*
Fresh sawdust	2.6	3.7
Birch shavings	1.7	0.8

* Mean of yields significantly greater than controls at the 5 percent level.

in the old barks than in fresh sawdust and shavings. If they had been compared directly with composted sawdust in this respect, the story might have been different (1).

Effects of Old Bark-Soil Mixtures
Without Fertilizer on Bean Yields

Old hardwood and old softwood bark were mixed each with soil in the proportion of ⅓ bark to ⅔ soil and Tiny wax beans grown in them in comparison to soil only as control. Fertilizer was omitted in order to determine something of the effects of the bark alone on plant growth. The plants were grown in ten-inch pots, with two plants per pot and twenty pots per treatment. The results in yield of seed appear in Table 4. The better yield of the plants grown in soil alone further strengthens the case

Table 4. Yields of Seeds of Wax Beans Grown in Soil-Bark Mixtures, No Fertilizer

	Soil Control	⅓ Old Hardwood Bark, ⅔ Soil	⅓ Old Softwood Bark, ⅔ Soil
Ave. No. of seeds from 20 plants	39.8	28.5	31.4
Ave. Wt. (grams) of seeds — 20 plants	17.2*	12.8	14.5

* Significantly greater than other yields at the 5 percent level.

that most of these organic soil supplements will not support or promote good plant growth without liberal amounts of fertilizer. This is still further emphasized and supported by the results on tomatoes given in the following section.

Effects on Tomato Yields of Pure Old Bark
Compared to Soil With Added Fertilizer

This was an experiment to determine something about the influence of bark alone (not mixed with soil) on plant growth. The two old barks were studied in comparison with pure peat, and with soil only as control. The materials were each placed in 10 glazed crocks of 2-gal. capacity. Before planting, 20 grams of 5-10-10 fertilizer was mixed with the contents of each crock. Young tomato plants of the New Hampshire Victor variety were transplanted, one to each container. Early in the course of this experiment all of the plants in pure peat died, evidently because of the low pH. Therefore, no yield data is available for the plants in this material. After the other plants had been growing for nearly two months 5 grams of ammonium nitrate were added to each crock as supplementary nutrient.

As the plants matured, records were kept of the yields of fresh ripe fruit from each plant. The yields are given in Table 5, as well as the average weight of the individual fruits from each material. The average yields for both bark treatments were considerably greater than for the soil con-

Table 5. Yields of Tomatoes Grown in Pure Bark Compared to Soil — Fertilizer Added

	Old Soft-wood Bark	Old Hard-wood Bark	Soil Control
Ave. yield of ripe fruits per plant (10 plants).	730.5	494.2	315.5
Ave. weight of individual fruits	60.3	62.5	45.7

trols, the one for the old softwood bark significantly so. The average size of fruits was considerably greater for each bark culture than the control. It appears from this that either one of the old barks makes an excellent growing medium, if an adequate nutrient supply is maintained.

Effect of Sewage Sludge on Growth of Plants in Bark

This experiment was conducted to determine something of the modifying effects of sewage sludge on bark as a growing medium. Sewage has been used extensively in Europe as a composting aid for various materials (2) and in composts with sawdust at this station (1). Two mixtures consisting of different proportions of sewage to the two kinds of old bark were prepared, namely, 1 to 5, and 1 to 8. No fertilizer was applied. Cabbage plants were grown in ten containers (one plant per container) of each of these mixtures in comparison to soil as a control. The yields are given in Table 6. The yield for each proportion of old hardwood bark to sewage is significantly greater than that from the soil controls. The plants in old softwood bark and sewage mixtures did not yield significantly greater than the plants in soil only.

Table 6. Dry Weight Yields of Cabbage (Tops) Grown in Bark-Sewage Mixtures and in Soil

Treatments	Mean Dry Wt. of 10 Plants
1 part sewage — 8 parts old hardwood bark	13.9*
1 part sewage — 5 parts old hardwood bark	11.6*
1 part sewage — 8 parts old softwood bark	7.2
1 part sewage — 5 parts old softwood bark	6.3
Soil — control	5.6

*Mean of yields significantly greater than controls at the 5 percent level.

Root Growth in Bark and Other Materials

The greenhouse operator, nurseryman, and other plantsmen are frequently concerned with growth of seedlings and getting a good start with them. It seemed desirable to secure information on seedling root growth in bark compared to other materials with which it might have to compete on the market.

The growth measurements of three kinds of seedlings, grown from seeds planted directly in the medium, are presented in Table 7. New softwood

Table 7. Comparative Tests of Root Growth in Bark and Other Materials

| | Root Lengths in Cm. — Mean of 10 Plants | | | | | |
| | Peas | | Onions | | Corn | |
Pure Materials	Tap Root	Lateral Root	Longest Root	Top Length	Tap Root	Side Root
Old hardwood bark	24.8	2.7	9.4	9.6	21.9	12.5
Old softwood bark	20.5	3.9	6.5	9.9	23.2	9.3
New softwood bark	12.6	2.8				
Sand	10.9	1.6	2.9	6.4	18.1	7.5
New hardwood bark	9.0	2.5				
Peat	3.3	1.1	2.7	9.7	14.3	8.2
Vermiculite			12.0	9.8	21.9	11.7

and new hardwood bark were somewhat adverse to the growth of seedling roots, mostly because they contained large pieces of bark which often blocked the penetration of roots. Also it is difficult to compact such coarse materials very much and roots are apt to dry out more readily in them. In general, root growth was best in all in the old barks. The only other material of those tried that compared favorably with the bark was fine vermiculite, tested for two kinds of seeds only.

Bark as a Rooting Medium for Cuttings

There is a continuing search for new and better media for rooting cuttings of various sorts. Since bark, especially the old materials, might offer possibilities here, a trial was made of old bark in comparison to sand. Beds in the basement at the greenhouse, furnished with fluorescent light, were prepared with the materials listed in Table 8. Concord grape cuttings were placed in them for over a month in early spring. The results on a limited number of cuttings show that old softwood bark, either alone or mixed with sand, has distinctly advantageous possibilities as a rooting medium.

Table 8. Comparison of Bark Mixtures as Rooting Media for Grape Cuttings

Rooting Media	Number Rooted	Percent Rooted
½ Old softwood bark, ½ sand	29	80
Old softwood bark	25	69
Sand	19	52
½ Old hardwood bark, ½ sand	18	50

Geranium cuttings rooted well in the two old barks mixed with sand, in comparison to sand alone. However, the roots broke off more easily in the sand-bark mixtures. This difficulty probably could be overcome by judicious watering.

Effects of Bark Mulches on Greenhouse Rose Production

Cow manure is widely used as mulch for greenhouse roses. It is not too readily available at times and waste bark seemed to offer some possibilities as a substitute. Two ground-beds of soil, 14 feet by 4 feet, were each divided in half, and each block prepared as follows: (a) received five 14-quart pails full of old hardwood bark, (b) 5 pails of peat, (c) nothing, (d) 5 pails old softwood bark. These additions were each mixed thoroughly with the soil and the beds steam sterilized. Eight hundred grams of superphosphate were then mixed with the contents of each block. Later, an equal number of two varieties of budded rose plants, Hildegarde and Better Times, were planted in the four blocks, 28 per block. Six hundred and eight grams of ground limestone were worked into the soil of each block. Three weeks later the following mulches were applied: block (a) a 3-4 inch layer of old hardwood bark, block (b) 3-4 inches of new hardwood bark, block (c) 3-4 inches of fresh cow manure, and block (d) 3-4 inches of old softwood bark.

During the course of the growth of these plants some trouble was experienced with black spot and insects but application of Fermate sprays and appropriate insecticides adequately controlled these troubles.

On May 6, about two and one-half months after setting out the plants, bloom started to appear. Two additional fertilizer applications were made during the summer. Late in August additional manure had to be added to block (c) because of the rapid breakdown of the mulch.

Careful records were taken of the yields of blooms, a summary of which appears in Table 9. These results show that both new or old bark makes an

Table 9. Yield of Roses with Bark and Manure Mulches

	Mulch Treatment			
	Old Hard- wood Bark	New Hard- wood Bark	Old Soft- wood Bark	Manure
Total no. of blooms	676	673	610	558
Ave. length of stems in inches	16.5	18.7	18.0	17.1

excellent mulch for roses. There is no significant difference between the total yields of 676 marketable roses for the old hardwood bark and 673 for the new hardwood bark, but the differences between these and 558 roses for the manure is probably significant.

The various mulch treatments caused no appreciable differences in stem lengths of the roses. All bark-mulched blocks produced stem lengths that would be regarded as adequate in the rose trade.

From the standpoint of working with the mulch in the greenhouse, the bark treatments, especially the new and old hardwood, are much easier to keep free of weeds. Also they do not decompose as rapidly as manure and thus do not need replacement as often.

There is a definite place for bark as a mulch in the rose industry. Corn cobs (ground up), tobacco stalks, and manure are some of the mulches now being used. The results of this experiment indicate that bark may well serve as a substitute for manure in mulching roses. It would last longer than many other materials.

Effect of Bark on Immunity of Apple to Scab

It had been suggested that apple trees grown all their lives in pure bark might be immune to the fungous disease known as apple scab. To test this hypothesis, ten crocks each of old hardwood bark, old softwood bark and soil control were each planted with five apple seeds. After germination, the seedlings were thinned to two per crock. Five grams of 5-10-10 fertilizer were added to each crock three times during growth. When the plants were about one foot high, they were artifically inoculated with the apple scab organism. Later observations showed severe scab infection on all bark grown plants and to the same extent as the soil controls. It is evident from this that growing apples in bark does not confer immunity to scab.

A Comparison of Shredded Bark and Sphagnum Peat As a Packing Material for Shipping Live Plants

The possibility of using waste bark as a material for keeping live plants moist naturally suggests itself. The bark was shredded by a hammer mill at the Brown Company plant in Berlin, New Hampshire. New bark was very stringy in comparison to the old bark.

A study was made of the comparative moisture holding capacity of shredded bark and peat. Each material was soaked over night in water.

Table 10. Moisture Retaining Power of Shredded Bark and Peat During Air-Drying

Date	Sphagnum Peat	Old Softwood Bark	Old Hardwood Bark	New Softwood Bark	New Hardwood Bark
		Weights in Grams			
7-7-52	1000	1000	1000	1000	1000
7-10	990	950	950	935	850
7-14	980	925	940	920	840
7-17	980	925	935	920	835
7-20	975	920	920	900	825
	Successive Weights of Oven Dried (80°C) Shredded Bark				
7-7-52		400	400	400	400
7-8		236	250	299	319
7-10		148	182	277	298
7-14		146	180	275	297
Percent water absorbed, dry wt. basis		174	122	45	34

11

They were then allowed to rest on a wire screen until gravitational water had drained away. One thousand grams of each moist substance were then used in a test of their power to retain water against air drying. Each mass of moist material was wrapped in polyethylene film with a ruler protruding from one end to simulate a plant stem and the possible loss of moisture through this seal. The results given in the upper part of Table 10 show that at the end of 13 days the peat retained more water than the bark. Also the old bark retained more water than the new bark.

The four shredded barks were tested for water loss in an oven to determine differences in rate of water loss at high temperature, also differences in water holding capacity on this basis. For a sample, 400 grams of water-soaked bark were used after drainage of gravitatural water. Samples were placed on paper squares in an oven at 80°C. Periodic weights were taken for one week, as presented in the lower part of Table 10. Thus it is shown the old bark had a much greater water retaining capacity than the new.

To test the effects on survival of living plants, nine rose plants were packed with each kind of bark and with peat. Polyethylene film was wrapped around the packing material. After the plants had been wrapped for a week and stored in a 60°F. greenhouse, observations were taken. For the first ten days the shredded bark kept the plants as healthy looking as did the peat. After the second week, the leaves of the old softwood treated roses showed a very slight wilting. At the end of the third week the peat-wrapped roses showed only a slight wilting while the old bark roses were quite wilted. Those in new shredded bark showed slightly more wilting than those in peat, but still looked vigorous. The above tests indicate that shredded bark may be used to good advantage as a moisture-holding packing material for shipping or storing live plants.

Part II   Field Plots

In order to determine the possible use of waste bark for improving field crop production, a field experiment was started on a plot of moderately level land in Madbury, New Hampshire. The soil type was Barnstead fine sandy loam and very uniform in texture. Soil samples showed an average pH of 5.2 and nutrients were present only in traces or were entirely lacking.

The total area, 140 feet x 300 feet, was divided into 30 plots 20 feet x 70 feet each. The treatments for the different series were:

1. No organic matter (control).
2. Manure, 1.5 tons per plot.
3. Old softwood bark, 120 cu. ft. per plot.
4. New softwood bark, 120 cu. ft. per plot.
5. Old hardwood bark, 120 cu. ft. per plot.
6. New hardwood bark, 120 cu. ft. per plot.

Each treatment was replicated five times in a randomized block design.

Five different crops were grown, as follows: (a) potatoes, Yampa the first year, and Kennebec the second year; (b) squash, Baby Blue; (c) beans, Jacobs Cattle; (d) bachelor button, *Centaurea cyanus*; and (e) zinnia, dahlia-flowered. One row of each of the crops was grown in each plot, running lengthwise of the plots, to facilitate cultivation.

Prior to planting and to bark or manure application, the entire area was plowed eight inches deep and harrowed thoroughly with a disk harrow. The old bark and manure were then mixed into the soil with a Gravely rotary plow. The new barks were left on the surface as a mulch. The details of planting and of fertilizer application will not be given here other than to state that what was considered to be ample fertilizer was applied. This was partly applied by machine placement at planting time and partly as side dressing later on. Each plot received the same amount of fertilizer, but considerably less fertilizer was applied to the rows of flower crops than to the vegetables.

In the fall of 1951, after the first crop was harvested, the new bark treatments were plowed under.

Cultivation during the growth of the crops was by hand hoeing, two men working almost continuously.

There was some deer damage to the bean and squash plants during growth, but an effort was made in presenting the harvest data to take that into account. The summer of 1952 was very dry, so that some of the later fertilizer applications were without effect.

Table 11. Yields of Crops Grown in Field Plots with Bark

Crops	Yields for Years	Old Soft-wood	Old Hard-wood	New Soft-wood	New Hard-wood	Control	Manure
Zinnia	1951	588	597	532	512	566	1612
	1952	2195	2035	1931	1893	1191	2120
No. of blooms totals		2783	2632	2463	2405	1757	3732
Bachelor button	1951	3705	2655	5774	7089	4295	14334
	1952	11700	13362	11610	9891	8126	17216
No. of blooms totals		15405	16017	17384	16980	12421	31550
Beans lbs. of pods	1951	56.6	66.0	51.7	54.2	22.3	97.2
	1952	107.1	86.5	76.6	69.8	53.7	103.8
	Totals	163.7	152.5	128.3	124.0	76.0	201.0
Squash lbs. of fruit	1951	564.0	710.3	721.7	619.8	554.0	979.7
	1952	309.9	240.3	251.1	236.7	238.9	232.8
	Totals	873.9	950.6	972.8	856.5	792.9	1212.5
Potatoes lbs. of tubers	1951	538	548	436	448	474	531
	1952	436	446	433	428	423	564
	Totals	974	994	869	876	897	1095

The total yield data for the different crops for each year and for both years together are summarized in Table 11. The totals for both years are shown graphically in Figure 1 in the order of size of yields for ready comparison.

Discussion of Field Plot Results

The zinnia harvest for the first year shows the manure plots to be the heaviest producers of flowers. The following year, the best yield was obtained with the old softwood bark, closely followed by manure and old hardwood. It should be noted, however, that all of the bark mixtures were ahead of the control in total production in 1952.

The bachelor button harvest for the first year showed the manure plots superior to all others. In the second year the manure was still the best medium, but the old softwood and hardwood bark mixtures were improved over 1951. There was better production the second year in the new bark plots when this material was plowed under than in the first year when it was used as a surface mulch.

The bark plots were probably starting to show some of the residual effects of the organic matter in the soil as reflected in the higher flower production in 1952 than in 1951. The new bark, when used as a mulch or plowed under, produced higher yields than the control. The high yields from the manure plots in both years shows that this is a satisfactory treatment for bachelor button production.

The bean harvest data show that the manure-treated plots yielded more than any other treatment in 1951. Statistical analysis could not be applied to the bean crop results because of the heavy deer damage. The results for 1952 compared to 1951, show that, as with the zinnias, the increase in yield in the old softwood bark plots was equal to that of the manure plots.

The Baby Blue squash yield in 1951 showed the manure plots again ahead of the other plots by a significant amount. The new bark plot yields indicate greater benefit from these when used as a mulch than when plowed under. In 1951 the manure plot yield was the only one significantly greater than controls at the 5 percent level. For 1952, when the yields for deer damaged plots are omitted, as presented here, the yields from the old softwood bark were outstandingly high. The others were close to the control.

With the potato crop in 1951, the yields for manure, old hardwood, and old softwood treatments were significantly greater than the controls at the 5 percent level. In 1952, the manure plot yield was the only one significantly greater.

In general the total yield data for all five crops, as shown in Figure 1, present two outstanding features. First, it is very obvious that the best yield for all crops was obtained with manure. This would be expected, for manure not only improves the physical qualities of soil, but also adds a considerable amount of plant nutrients beyond those supplied by the regular fertilizer treatments. It is well recognized that bark would add scarcely any of these elements. The other noteworthy feature is that all four of the bark treatments gave greater total yields than the control with all crops except the potato. This indicates that bark has some potentialities as a soil improver.

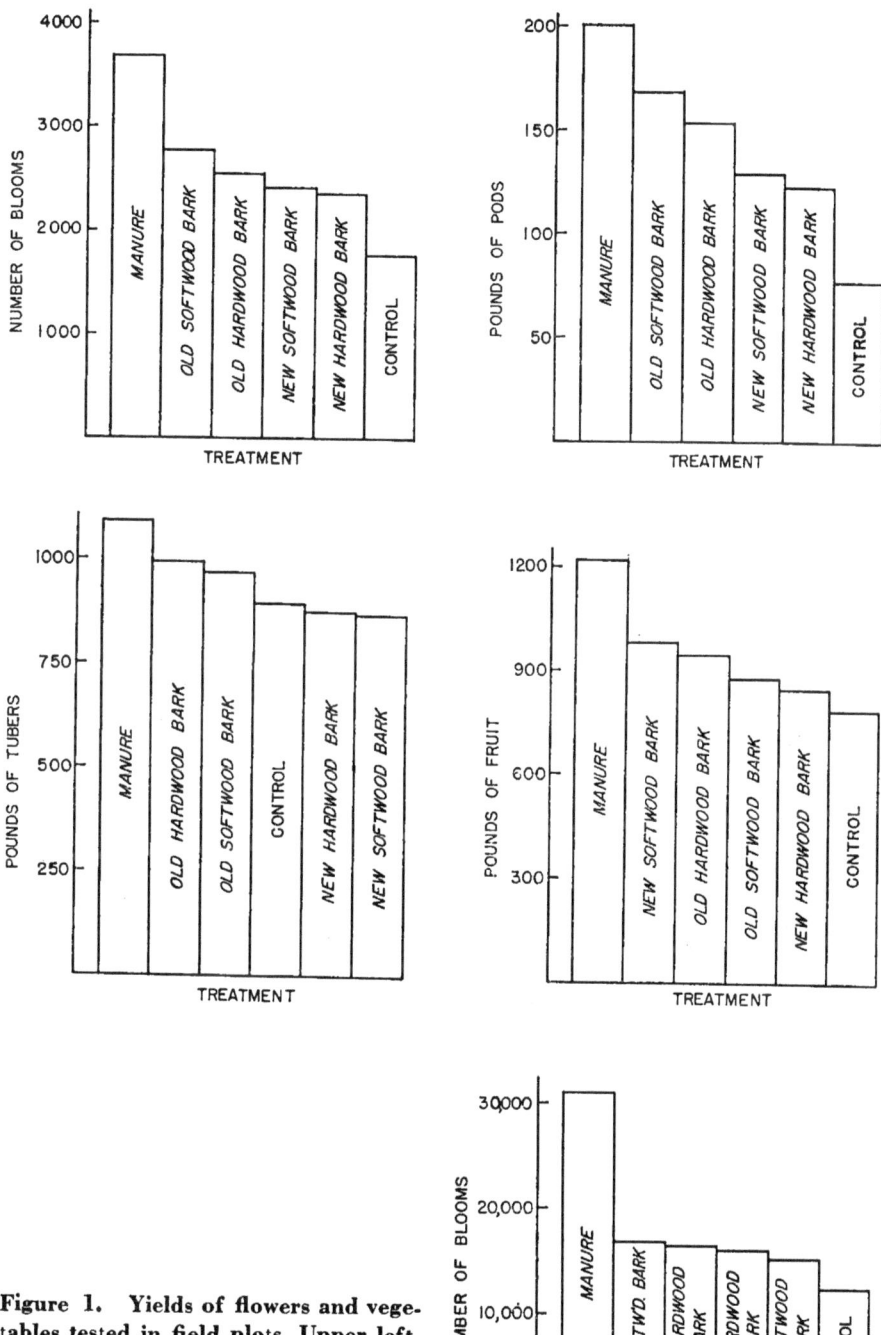

Figure 1. Yields of flowers and vegetables tested in field plots. Upper left, zinnias; upper right, beans; middle left, potato tubers; middle right, squash; lower right, bachelor buttons.

Summary

This is a report on experiments to determine the possible value of waste bark as a soil improver. The bark was used in greenhouse cultures with plants and in field plot tests.

In the greenhouse, the effect of bark on plant growth was tested both in mixtures with soil and in the pure state. Both pot and bed cultures were employed. Usually it was compared with soil alone as control cultures, and often with peat under similar conditions. The greenhouse experiments comprise nine sets of cultures, and one of tests of water holding capacity.

1. A set of pot cultures designed to show the effects on plant growth of varying proportions of bark to soil, and peat to soil, showed that low concentrations of these organic substances gave better yields than higher ones. Older bark gave higher yields than fresh ones and peat for the first crop (cabbage) and significantly higher yields than soil controls. However, advantages for these additives tended to disappear with successive crops (radish and corn), probably due to decay of the organic matter.

2. Flower yields of two ornamentals were tested in greenhouse bench cultures with (a) old bark-soil mixture, (b) peat-soil, and (c) soil only. With snapdragons the yield was best in bark and next best in peat. Carnations yielded best in the peat mixture. However, none of the differences were very great, probably due to high compost content of the original soil.

3. Old bark, undiluted with soil but with added fertilizer, was compared with other wood wastes and soil as growing media for cabbage and barley. Yields for both in bark was significantly greater than in soil.

4. Even old bark will not increase yields of plants in bark-soil mixtures above that of soil controls, unless fertilizer is added. This was demonstrated by growing wax beans in a one-to-two ratio of bark to soil, with no fertilizer. The yield from soil-grown plants was significantly greater.

5. The statements in 3 and 4 above were further substantiated by results with tomatoes grown in pure old bark in comparison with pure peat and soil. Each was liberally fertilized. The crop in peat was a total failure. Total yields of fruit, as well as size of fruit, was greater in the bark than in soil by a very wide margin.

6. Pot cultures of cabbage were grown in mixtures of old bark and sewage sludge (no added fertilizer), in comparison to soil. The old hardwood bark-sewage mixtures produced significantly better growth than did soil. Yields in those of old softwood bark were close to yields of the controls.

7. The root growth of three kinds of seedlings in the four kinds of bark was compared with root growth in other kinds of media, such as sand. Growth was best in old bark, but that in vermiculite was about as good for two kinds of seedlings.

8. Tests of old bark, alone and mixed with sand, as rooting media for grape cuttings showed that these media have good possibilities for such use. Bark was also satisfactory for rooting geranium.

9. Used as a mulch for growing greenhouse roses, bark showed outstanding possibilities. Yields of rose blooms were considerably greater with two bark mulches than when mulched with cow manure. The bark also lasted longer than manure.

10. Bark as a growing medium for apple seedlings had no influence on infection from scab. This was contrary to a supposition that it might cause immunity.

11. Shredded bark compared very favorably with sphagnum peat as a packing material for live plants.

For field plot trials, the four kinds of bark, in comparison to manure and controls without organic matter, were applied in replicated plots. All were fertilized alike. As might be expected from the additional fertility it contained (beyond the commercial fertilizer application), manure produced best yields for all five crops tested. However, plants grown in the two kinds of old bark produced considerably higher yields than those in the soil controls in 8 out of a possible 10 cases. Even the new barks gave higher yields than controls with all crops except potatoes. When it is considered that the original soil was practically devoid of nutrients, this shows that bark has considerable potentialities as a soil builder in field use.

Literature Cited

1. BAKER, J. R., AND DUNN, S. Sawdust Composts in Soil Improvement: III. Pot Culture Studies with Composts from (a) Outdoor Pits (b) Wooden Bins with High Moisture, (c) Other Mixtures. Plant and Soil 6:113-128. 1955.

2. Composting for Disposal of Organic Refuse, and Biblography. Techn. Bul. 1 and 2, Institute of Eng. Res., Univ. of Calif., 1950.

3. DUNN, S., WOLFE, L. P. JR., MacDONALD, W. A., AND BAKER, J. R. Field Plot Studies with Sawdust for Soil Improvement. *Plant and Soil* 4:164-170. 1952.

4. MacDONALD, W. A., AND DUNN, S. Sawdust Composts in Soil Improvement: II. Pot Cultures with Compost Mixtures of Sawdust and Manure, Steam Treated Composts and Miscellaneous Mixtures. *Plant and Soil* 4:235-247. 1953.

5. Northeastern Wood Utilization Council Inc., The Chemistry and Utilization of Bark. Bulletin 25. 1949.

6. RETTIE, J. C., AND SIMMONS, F. C. Estimates of Bark Supply in the Northeast. In Northeastern Wood Utilization Council Bul. 25:7-18. 1949.

7. WOLFE, L. P. JR., AND DUNN, S. Sawdust Composts in Soil Improvement: I. Studies on Aeration, Acid Hydrolysis, Manure and Waste Materials as Composting Aids. *Plant and Soil* 4:223-234. 1953.

The Comparative Value of Bark as a Surface Mulch for Apples, Blueberries, and Raspberries

By L. PHELPS LATIMER

Associate Horticulturist
New Hampshire Agricultural Experiment Station

Apples

IT is standard orchard practice in the New England states to grow apple trees under a sod-mulch system, placing additional hay or other suitable mulching materials on the ground beneath the spread of the branches of the trees in order to control weed growth, improve the physical condition of the soil, conserve moisture, and supply mineral nutrients. Cultivation is thus eliminated. Hay has been considered the best material for this purpose.

The purpose of this experiment was to determine the value of bark compared to hay as a mulching material in the orchard. Three separate blocks of trees were utilized, and the tests were started in the autumn of 1950 as follows:

1. 32 five-year-old McIntosh at Durham.

2. 25 seven-year-old McIntosh at Durham.

3. 120 three-year-old Virginia Crab and Robusta No. 5 apple stocks at West Stewartstown.

In the experiment at Durham, old softwood bark was compared with hay as mulch; at West Stewartstown, old softwood bark and new softwood bark were compared with hay as mulch. The criteria for measuring the response to different mulches were annual twig growth in all blocks and, in addition, yield of fruit in Block 1 (at Durham).

Since the difference in twig growth between treatments was not stastically significant at the 5 percent level, the data taken at Durham indicate that the bark-mulched trees compared favorably with hay-mulched trees in terminal growth. At West Stewartstown there seemed to be a tendency for hay-mulched trees to make slightly greater terminal growth than those mulched with either new or old softwood bark. On the other hand, trees mulched with old softwood bark made growth equal to that produced by trees mulched with new softwood bark.

Results comparing yields are not conclusive; first, because the trees were only bearing their first small crops, and second, because mulch placed around the trees in the fall of 1950 could not possibly have had an effect on fruit bud formation until the summer of 1951, and consequently on the fruit crop of 1952. Further observations are needed for definite conclusions.

Blueberries

On October 16, 1950, plots were set up on the Chandler Farm in Dover to compare the effects of new hardwood bark, old softwood bark, sawdust, and hay on annual shoot growth of blueberries. The growth made by plants mulched with new hardwood bark as well as by those mulched with hay was significantly greater at the 1 percent level than the growth made by plants mulched with old softwood bark, and was significantly greater at the 5 percent level than growth made by plants mulched with sawdust. The fact that the least growth was made by blueberry plants mulched with old softwood bark may be reflected in the fact that there was less soil nitrate nitrogen beneath the old softwood bark than under the new hardwood-bark mulch. One apparent advantage of the bark mulches is that these materials are free from the seeds of obnoxious weeds.

At the Smith Farm in Gilford, three-year-old blueberry plants were mulched in the fall of 1950, some with old hardwood bark, and some with hay. A control row was kept in clean cultivation. In the winter of 1950-51, heavy snow broke down the blueberry plants to the ground. The hay-mulched and clean-cultivated plants did not recover, whereas the plants mulched with old hardwood bark did recover and performed well subsequently. The bark mulch appeared to be superior to any other for blueberries. It was very easy to work and to keep free of witch grass and other weeds.

Raspberries

Four 150-foot rows of Durham fall-bearing raspberries at the University Horticultural Farm were used for this experiment. One row was kept in cultivation, one mulched with hay, one with sawdust and one with old softwood bark. The results showed that the cultivated row outyielded the rows under mulch treatments.

The bark-mulched row, however, produced more fruit than the hay or sawdust-mulched rows. The largest sized berries were produced on plants mulched with either sawdust or hay. This probably was the result of lower yield under these treatments. More sucker plants were produced in the bark-mulched row than in the other rows. This might be an advantage to the commercial nurseryman.

Shipment ID _UNH 02/19/08____

Item #s   _124.01 - 124.25_____

This bound volume contains more than one item.

Divide here for _124.11_____

See loader or manager w/ any questions.

APRIL 1957

:TS

9 781334 267772